freaky FUN activities

jay stephens

IMPACT
CINCINNATI, OHIO
www.impact-books.com

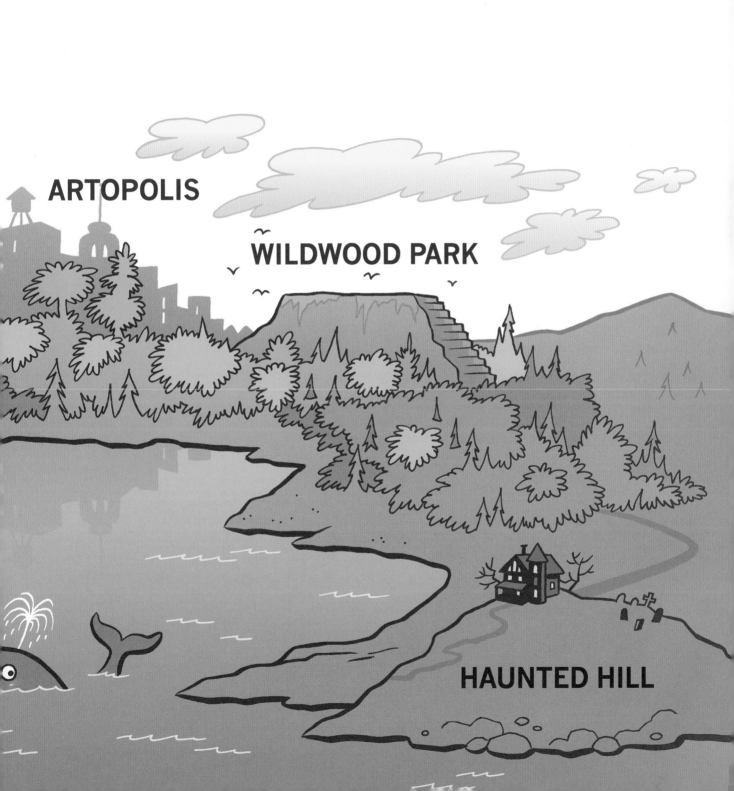

Contents

 Visit impact-books.com/freakyfunactivities to download a free bonus demonstration.

Welcome to Artopolis!

Artopolis is a place where anything you create comes to life! If you can draw it, make it or color it, it will have a place to live in this imaginative, artistic, very silly city. We may need your help to solve some problems, and nothing beats a problem like creativity!

So come on in and explore a place where mixed-up animals, wandering robots, goofy ghosts, far-out space creatures and super-hero doodles are waiting to welcome you. All you need to bring is your imagination and something to sketch with.

5

What You'll Need

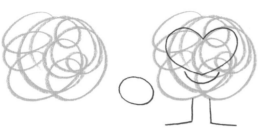

Hi, my name is Scribble! How doodle you do? Here are the things you need to play with us in ARTOPOLIS…

An erasable pencil

A fine-tip black marker or black pen

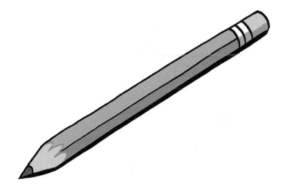

Lots of colored markers, colored pencils or crayons

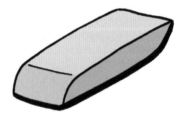

An eraser

A ruler

Visit impact-books.com/freakyfunactivities to download a free bonus activity.

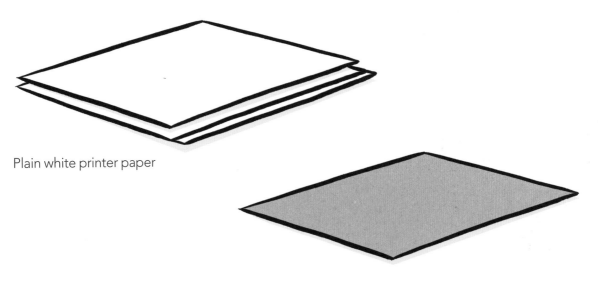

Plain white printer paper

Thin cardboard, like the kind from cereal boxes

Glue and tape

Washable paint—tempera paint is best.

A pair of scissors—be careful!

Additional Supplies

The items shown here are the most important, but for a few projects you will also need: kitchen utensils, wax paper, construction paper, string, a paper plate and a craft knife. (Be sure to have an adult help you with the craft knife!)

Draw It!

DoodleBug

Uh-oh! Some strange disaster has happened in the City of Artopolis! Can you help me? We need my partner, DoodleBug, to help us solve the mystery. Follow the steps to make the city's greatest super-hero appear.

1 Using an erasable pencil, sketch an oval shape on top of two stacked oblong shapes. Notice they are thinner where they meet in the middle. At this stage, it's important to draw everything lightly.

2 Add two teardrop shapes to the top of the oval and two short lines angled downward inside the oval. Draw one line through the middle of the two oblongs. Draw another line crossing that one and extending through the middle of the top oblong shape. Create the toes and arms with simple angles that look like the letter V.

3 Create DoodleBug's eyes and smile with curved U shapes. Use gentle curves to make the tops of his gloves and boots, and two bigger curved J shapes for his cape. Sketch two circles on either side of the crossed lines on his chest. Then draw two smaller circles inside of those. Begin his fists with small rectangles.

Visit impact-books.com/freakyfunactivities to download a free bonus activity.

4 Add two short lines for the neck and two more short lines above the circles on his chest. Use three lines to divide up the fingers and three more lines for each thumb.

5 Erase any extra parts you don't need for the final drawing. Use a black pen or marker to ink the sketch by tracing the lines you have roughed out. Now you have a clean final version.

6 Add color with markers, colored pencils or crayons. This is how DoodleBug usually looks...

7 However, someone has attacked Artopolis, and this is how DoodleBug looks right now. Draw his torn costume using V shapes. You can draw simple dirty scrapes by sketching three short lines crossing on top of three more short lines. Long wavy lines look like steam, and boy is DoodleBug ever steamed! His smile is upside down now. I think he should go change into a new costume before we turn the page, don't you?

Make It!

Kitchen Print City

The first thing DoodleBug and Scribble would like to do is rebuild the damaged city of Artopolis. You can help them remake the city using items in your kitchen. So clear some counter space—we're going to make a bit of a mess with tempera paint.

1 Fill a jar or glass with water and tape a piece of wax paper to the counter top. Spread any color paint you like onto the wax paper. Add some water to keep it moist. Press a metal or plastic kitchen utensil straight down into the paint. Then press it onto a piece of regular white paper, leaving a paint stamp.

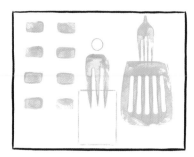

2 Make stamps out of a few other items, making sure to always go straight up and down off the paper so you don't smear the prints. Add water or more paint if it starts to get too dry. The utensils used in this example are: the bottom of an ice-cube tray, a hot-sauce cap, a big salad fork, the bottom of a cheese grater, a regular fork and spatula.

3 Once the paint is dry, use a ruler and pen to add some straight lines. If you like, use markers, colored pencils or crayons to add more color and details to your city street.

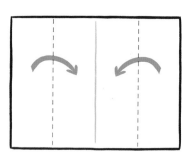

4 Now we need to stand those buildings up! Fold a regular sheet of white paper in half. Open the sheet back up, and then fold each side in so the edges meet at the center fold line.

5 Stand the paper up, tuck one end behind the other to form a triangular end, and then tape or glue it together.

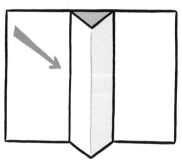

6 Tape or glue the stand onto the back of your city design. Make a second one if you want a stronger support at each end.

Visit impact-books.com/freakyfunactivities to download a free bonus activity.

7 To bring life back to the streets, carefully cut out the Artopolis citizens below. Fold back the base stands on the dotted lines, and stand them up in front of your cityscape. Joining DoodleBug and Scribble are Malcolm McGhool, Doctor NoGo and Fourbot.

Solve It!

Invisible Aid

Redraw the invisible thing on the opposite page by completing the double dot-to-dots. First, start on the arrow point and connect the numbered dots from 1 to 100 with a pencil, pen or marker. Next, find letter A and connect the lettered dots in alphabetical order from A to Z. What do you see?

MATERIALS

pencil, pen or marker

12

Color It!

Go Green

Have you ever colored a picture all with one color? The invisible creature has sent you to Wildwood Park in pursuit of a mystery villain. It's on the outskirts of the city where there are lots of trees. The park is usually very green, but seven different kinds of green! However, someone has drained all the color from Wildwood and we need you to match the different green colors to the swatches below to bring life back to the parkland.

LIME For the flowers, Mea Moth, Fancy Frog, Squishquatch, Bird beak, T-rex and serpent eyes

APPLE For all trees and bushes with rounded leaves, Goofy Apple, Gnome face, ears, and hands, and T-rex tongue

LAUREL For the clouds, rocks and the bridge

PINE For all trees and bushes with spiky leaves, Smiley Serpent, and T-rex's cheek

MINT For the sky and the Chilly Bird

HUNTER For the T-rex, Gnome's hat and hair, and Creek

OLIVE For Bog Boy, the hills, and the gnome's shoulder

Draw It!

Guardin' Gnome

Normally this little dude helps DoodleBug and Scribble by protecting the forests and hills outside of downtown. Something is wrong with the Wildwood, however, and he's so upset he is hiding! Help make the gnome appear by following the steps to draw him.

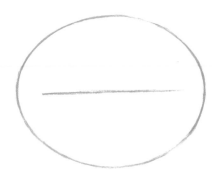

1 Sketch an oval, then draw a line in the middle. Remember to sketch lightly with an erasable pencil so you can easily fix little mistakes and clean up your rough sketch at the end.

2 Add some C shapes—two for the ears and two for the eyes.

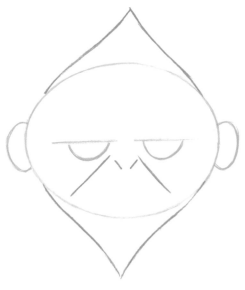

3 Draw two slightly curved V shapes to create his hat and beard. Sketch two short angled lines create his nose, and two longer lines make grumpy wrinkles.

Visit impact-books.com/freakyfunactivities to download a free bonus activity.

4 Create a frown with another gentle C shape. Draw a longer C shape for his forehead wrinkle and two small ones for eyebrows. Sketch three C's in a row to make bushy sideburns beside each ear. Add four tilting W shapes for spiky hair.

5 Connect the W shapes with long C shapes beside the ears and with short lines to the bushy sideburns. Add tiny circles to the eyes to make pupils, and two short lines between his eyebrows to make him look even grumpier. Carefully erase any unnecessary rough lines.

6 Ink your drawing by tracing it with a dark pen or marker, then color in your gnome with some sour greens. DoodleBug wants the Guardin' Gnome to help him find the villain who has been messing around with Artopolis, but he needs to cheer him up first. Can you figure out how to make the Guardin' Gnome smile? I'll give you a hint—you need to turn that frown upside down!

Solve It!

Mid-Forest Double Cross

The Gnome says the mysterious meanie went this-a-way! The trail through the middle of the forest is very dangerous. One wrong move and you could fall into the scary caves below. Help DoodleBug and Scribble solve this challenging puzzle to get to the other side. First, you must solve the crossword. You don't need to solve the answers in order—any answer will give you a clue to the words it overlaps, so start with the answers you're pretty sure of.

ACROSS

2 E.T. is short for another word for aliens
8 The big prehistoric creature from page 15
9 He's the spitting ___ of his father!
10 The absolute most allowed
12 Something you've made is your ___
15 Clever ___ a fox
16 Pythons, chinchillas and capuchin monkeys are ___ pets
19 A light wind
21 Slippery, snake-like water creature
22 A car needs a regular ___ change
23 A boat ___ on top of the water
25 Itchy red spots mean you might have this illness
27 The shortest way to write "hug, kiss, hug, kiss, hug"
28 The opposite of hit
30 I was so hungry I ___ the whole pizza!
31 Which came first, the chicken or the ___?
32 Digital images are also called computer ___
34 A big hunk of wood for your fire
35 Opposite of stop
37 Fairs, shows or exhibits
38 When no one can say what really happened, it remains ___
40 Opposite of off
41 At Halloween, not Treated, but ___
44 Colored stone, often black
46 In summer, it's usually OK to ___ your friends with water
47 A house for chickens
49 He was fifteen-and-three-quarters, and looking forward to his ___ birthday
51 If mom says no, go ask your ___
52 Sports cars, jewelry and designer clothes are ___ items
53 A wheeled wooden vehicle pulled by 36 down

DOWN

1 Sleek water mammal
2 When you're extinct, you cease to ___
3 The number of years your friends have been around are their ___
4 The ways out of places
5 Stir up ingredients again
6 You can ___ a pet from an animal shelter
7 Rare and hard to find anywhere
10 Where mailed letters are delivered
13 It chops wood
14 To blow a story wayyyy out of proportion
15 The rod between two wheels
20 "My dog ate it" is a bad one
23 Wild, orange-colored canines
24 Something you have to read from at school
25 The opposite of simple
26 Things that thrill you and get you worked up
29 Ancient Egyptian lion with a human head
33 When you cease to exist, you are ___
36 A cow-like animal used for pulling things
38 Still broken
39 Legendary bird that burns up and is reborn
41 Black suit and bow tie
42 A professional
43 Tentacled sea creature
45 Opposite of no
48 ___ my gosh!
50 Cold and slippery

Now that you've solved the crossword, can you guide DoodleBug and Scribble through the maze without them stepping on any X squares? X marks the spots where the trail is too deadly to pass. (Answers on page 60.)

Visit impact-books.com/freakyfunactivities to download a free bonus activity.

Make It!

Screechy Owl

DoodleBug and Scribble see an owl that looks like he knows something. Can you follow the steps here to get him to talk?

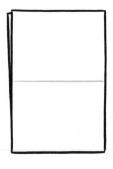

1 Take a sheet of 8 ½" × 11" (22cm × 28cm) white paper and fold it in half. Unfold it and then fold it in half the other way. It should look like this.

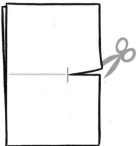

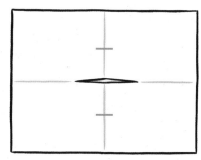

2 Use a ruler to mark a spot with a pencil 2 inches (5cm) in from the folded side along the fold mark. Carefully cut up to that mark with scissors. Unfold the paper. Measure with a ruler and mark with a pencil two spots, both 2 inches (5cm) up and down from the cut line along the fold line, as shown.

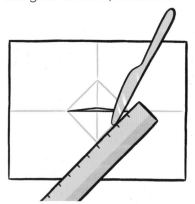

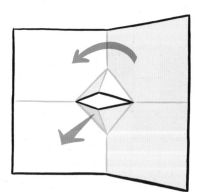

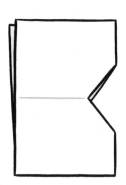

3 Make sure your paper is on a hard surface. Draw a light line connecting the edges of the cut line to the spots you measured. Use a ruler to keep your lines straight. Trace this diamond shape with the back of a table knife or butter knife (nothing sharp!). Press down with the knife to score the paper, leaving a creased, dented line. Fold the paper back over as shown, this time gently pulling the beak parts forward as you fold it in half. The beak should fold along the lines you scored into the paper.

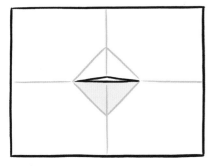

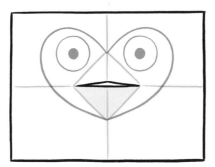

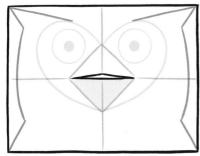

4 Unfold the paper. Lightly sketch a heart shape with the points touching the top and bottom of the beak. Draw two circles for eyes with big pupils inside the eyes. Draw two V shapes from the top of the heart shape out to the corner of the paper and back in a short distance. Draw two short lines inward diagonally from the bottom corners. Now connect the top and bottom angled lines with very gently curved lines. Sketch more V shapes to make the tip of his beak and add some zig-zag lines to create fluffy feathers.

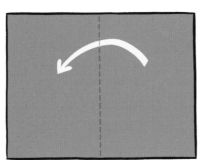

5 Time to ink your owl face with a dark pen, marker, colored pencil or crayon. Erase your rough pencil lines. Color in the face using the example here or any colors you like. Now take a new sheet of paper and color one side of it red. Fold it in half, then glue or tape the owl face onto the red paper. Be careful not to glue the part with the moving beak! When the glue is dry, carefully cut out the edges around the owl head. Now your screetchy owl can talk his head off!

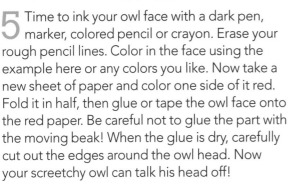

21

Color It!

Right There in Black and White

The Screechy Owl has given DoodleBug some clues as to who's behind messing up all of Artopolis, but owl-language is hard to understand. He has put all the information into his portable Doodle-computer and printed off this mysterious graphic. The answer is hiding within its abstract lines and shapes. Which naughty citizen is behind the mess?

MATERIALS

black, dark gray and light gray colored pencils or markers

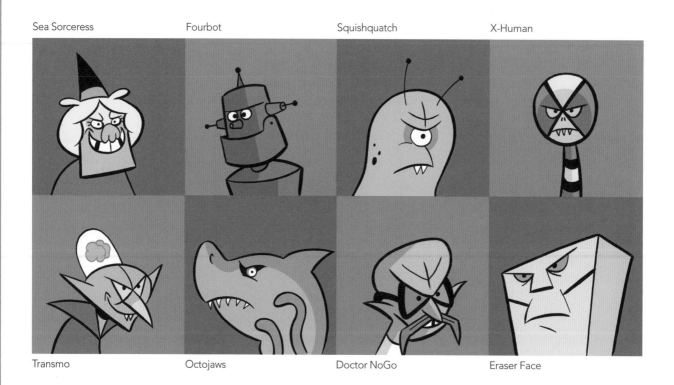

Sea Sorceress Fourbot Squishquatch X-Human

Transmo Octojaws Doctor NoGo Eraser Face

Have you ever colored a picture with just black, white and gray? Try to match the samples here with pencil crayons or markers, and help DoodleBug and Scribble reveal the culprit. Color in the shapes marked with an L light gray. Color in the shapes marked with a D dark gray. Leave the shapes marked with a W white. Color in the shapes marked with a B black. (Answers on page 60.)

23

Draw It!

Zompanzie

Ah-ha! Thank you for helping DoodleBug and Scribble figure out which sneaky scoundrel is responsible for messing everything up! That certainly explains the strange transformations we've seen so far. And here comes another mixed-up weirdo right now—a zompanzie!

1 Draw one oval for his head and a tilted egg shape for his body. Notice that the egg is off to the side a little. Remember not to press too hard so it's easier to erase later on.

2 Use another oval to create a snout. Add two circles above it to make eyes. Draw the arms with two curved lines, side-by-side. Make both legs a set of side-by-side curved lines, like a bridge.

3 Draw two more ovals for the hands. Use two more flatter ovals to make the chimp's feet. Outline his ears, smile and cheeks with C-shaped curves. Use two more circles to create his big pupils. Draw short lines for his eyebrows, nostrils and under the eyes. Cute, huh?

4 Sketch V shapes to make his kooky hairdo, adding chest hair and scruff at the back of his neck. Finish his ears and top lip with tiny curves. Create the fingers with three curved lines on each hand, and two more of these same curved lines on each foot to make toes. Draw a big toe on each foot with an almost-oval shape.

5 Erase the unneeded pencil lines and ink the chimp by tracing the sketch with a black marker or pen. Add color with colored pencils, markers or crayons.

6 Instead of inking and coloring, go straight from step 4 to here. Erase his big adorable pupils and replace them with two little circles to make crooked, beady, googly eyes. Erase his smile and create a gaping mouth with a wavy line and U shapes. Monster stitches are made with a line crossed by two or three shorter lines. Add some dots for yucky blotches. Add flies by drawing a black oval with two little teardrop shapes for wings. Sketch slotted, wiggly lines to show them flying around. Erase one of his arms and draw an oval to show where it came off.

7 Color the zombie version with icky colors. He's gross, but still kind of cute!

Solve It!

Haunted Hall Mix-Up

Transmo's trail of transformation leads right to the creaky doors of Haunted Hall. The ghosts who make their home here are normally restless, but DoodleBug has never seen them like this! They are so distracted by all the little changes the villain made that they can't help DoodleBug and Scribble find him until they've settled down.

26

Can you help spot thirteen differences between the two pictures below to calm the spirits?
(Answers on page 61.)

Phantobat

Transmo frightened all the pet Phantobats away from Haunted Hall. You can help DoodleBug and Scribble get on Captain A. Ghast's good side by creating some more. Here's how to make a Phantobat...

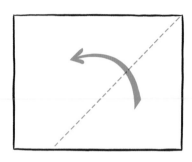
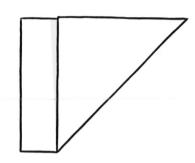
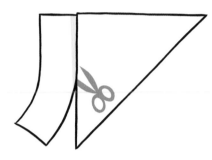

1 Take a piece of standard 8 ½" × 11" (22cm × 28cm) white printer paper and fold up one corner as shown so it looks like this. Now carefully trim off the edge with scissors.

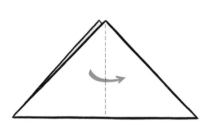
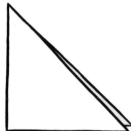
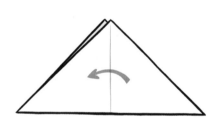

2 Turn the triangle of paper so the folded edge is at the bottom. Now fold it in half so it looks like this. Unfold it again.

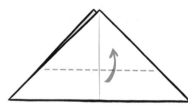
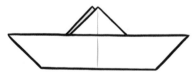

3 Fold up the bottom at around 2" (5cm). You can use a ruler so it looks like this.

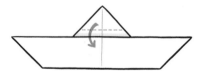

4 Fold down the top at around ½" (1.3cm). Draw two eyes with colored pencils or markers, and use scissors to carefully trim out the little triangular shapes.

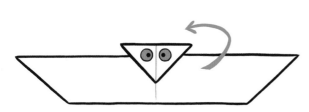  

5 Now fold it in half backwards. Next, fold both wings up along the dotted lines.

 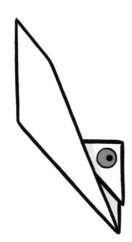 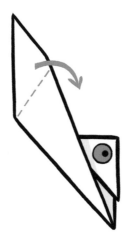 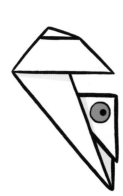

6 Fold both wings back along the dotted lines. Now fold the wing tips down along the dotted lines.

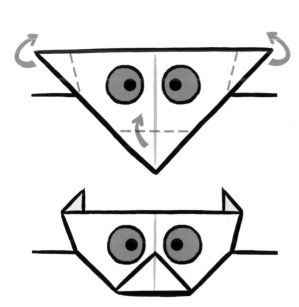

7 Unfold the Phantobat to finish its face. Fold back the two ears, and fold up the lower jaw.

You can make a bunch of bats with different colors and faces!

Color It!

Feeling Blue

Haunted Hall's owner, Captain A. Ghast has sent one of his ghost guests, Boo-Hoo, to show you the way Transmo went—to the bottom of Boggy Bay! Here's another picture to color. Transmo has drained all the beautiful blues from Boggy Bay, and it's making the folks who live there kind of sad. It's usually seven different kinds of blue! Match markers or pencil crayons to the color swatches below to spruce up the bay.

MATERIALS

colored pencils, markers or crayons in various shades of blue

POWDER For the distant hills, Boo-Hoo Ghost's tear and the sandy bottom with dots

TEAL For the water and the starfish

IRIS For J.J. Blue Jay, Fourbot and the small fish

TURQUOISE For Haunted Hill, Bog Boy, the turtle's head, the big fish and the sandy bottom with no dots

AZURE For the underwater cliffs and the turtle's body

CERULEAN For the sky, Bubba Blue Whale and Boo-Hoo Ghost's pupils

COBALT For Haunted Hall, the shipwreck and the crab

Draw It!

Sea Sorceress

Someone in Boggy Bay still seems quite out of sorts. The Sea Sorceress isn't such a bad person, really. She simply isn't feeling herself. Let's see if we can find a creative solution to her problem. (Solution on page 61.)

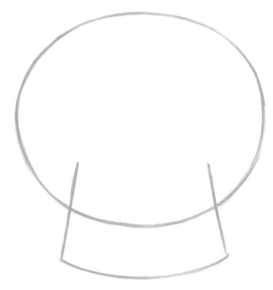

1 Draw a circle. Sketch two straight, slightly angled lines and one curved line. Connect them to create the jaw.

2 Draw a big tulip-shaped nose. The bottom part should have three bumps that rest on the bottom of the circle. Sketch two oval eye shapes. Draw a curved line for her forehead.

3 Draw two J shapes at the top of the head and, a C shape above each eye. Add a pair of short curved lines under each eye. Draw two curved V shapes to make the frown.

32

4 Draw another V shape to make the witch hat. Draw two C shapes to finish off her poofy hairdo. Use a zig-zag line to make her forehead wrinkle up in a worried way. Create the bridge of her nose with a curved L shape.

5 Add some little circles for pupils, small curled lines for eyelashes and short lines for teeth.

6 Erase any lines you don't need anymore and ink your sketch with a black pen or marker. Color in your Sea Sorceress any way you like with colored pencils, markers or crayons. Take a good look at her. She seems so worried, doesn't she? How can Doodle-Bug change her into a happier person? Maybe a fresh perspective is all that's needed. Turn the page upside down to view this problem from another angle.

Solve It!

Mysterious Threat

As DoodleBug and Scribble set off across the Bay at dusk, something sinister awaits them. Solve the double connect-the-dots puzzle by joining dots in order from A to Z and then from 1 to 195 to discover a secret threat!

MATERIALS

pencil, pen or marker

Shark-Tooth Trophy

It turns out that OctoJaws is all snaggle and no tooth! His scary-looking chompers are fake! OJ wants to apologize for frightening everyone, and is offering his scary-looking shark teeth as a trophy for DoodleBug to keep. Follow the steps to make a set of jaws of your own.

  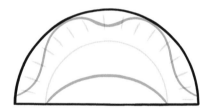

1 Fold the bottom of a paper plate in half as shown. Draw a downward-curved line at the fold. Then draw a wavy shape around the upper edge of the plate—like an M in the middle with S shapes at the sides.

 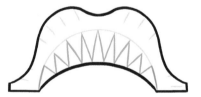 

2 Use scissors to carefully trim away the pieces you drew. Sketch a zig-zag with as many fangs as you like. Make sure the drawing starts and ends at the edges of the cut-out curve at the folded edge. Then carefully cut out the teeth with scissors.

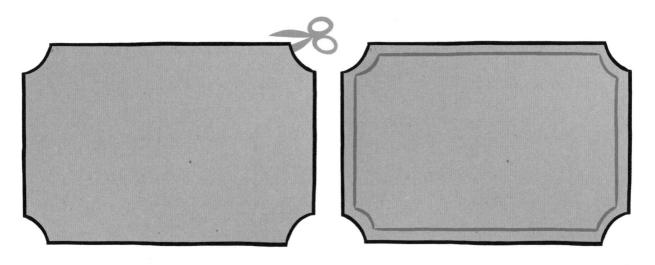

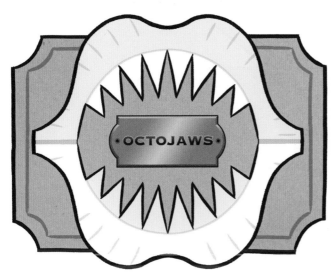

3 Trim the corners off a piece of cardboard with curved shapes as shown. The back of a cereal box or large frozen food box works well. Trace a line all the way around with a brown marker or crayon. Open up your shark jaws. Fold the teeth out a little so they stick out in a menacing way. Tape or glue the bottom hinge of the jaws to the cardboard plaque so the top still opens and closes. Carefully cut out the brass plate below and finish off by gluing or taping it to the middle of the plaque. What a crazy souvenir!

37

Color It!

Where's Scribble?

The waters are rough on Boggy Bay, and big waves rock the boat, sending poor Scribble shooting off into the air! Where did he go?

MATERIALS

colored pencils, markers or crayons in black and various shades of gray

Have you ever colored a picture with just black, white and gray? Help DoodleBug discover where Scribble went by matching the samples here with colored pencil, crayons or markers. Color in the shapes marked with an L light gray. Color in the shapes marked with a D dark gray. Leave the blank shapes white. Color in the shapes marked with a B black. (Solution on page 61.)

Draw It!

Cat + Frog = Crog

The first thing to greet DoodleBug and Scribble as they arrive on Volcano Point is another one of Transmo's weirdly transformed creatures— a creepy CROG! Can you help these poor critters become more like themselves by redrawing them the regular way?

1 Draw an oval with a curved line off to one side to begin your frog's head and body.

2 Use C shapes to create the brim of his hat, the eye on the side and his back knee. Draw a circle for the other eye. Sketch V shapes for his front legs. Draw the smile with a J shape and a little line underneath for the chin.

3 Draw a line to complete the top hat, and an X with little lines closing off each end to make a matching bow-tie. Add a little oval for the pupil. use connected U shapes to create the fingers and toes.

4 Ink, erase and color!

5 Begin Lickety Kitten with an oval head. Add a U shape off to one side to make the body. Sketch cat ears with two upside-down V shapes.

6 Add oval eyes, a triangle nose and an upside-down M for the mouth. Sketch another M shape for her back leg. Make the top leg with two U shapes connected at the paw. Draw two straight lines with a C shape for a paw to create the bottom legs.

7 Draw the tail and tongue with J shapes. Use little lines to make the toes and pupils. Use longer lines for whiskers and add three dots on each cheek.

8 Ink, erase and color!

Solve It!

Tricky Eye-Twisters

Transmo has created some optical illusions to slow down DoodleBug!
Can you help sort out this tricky business? (Answers on page 62.)

Which square is bigger: A or B?

Which green line between the arrows is the longest: A, B or C?

In Transmo's world, sometimes a candlestick is also two people talking!

I'm two things at once—a DuckBunny from Transmo's dimension!

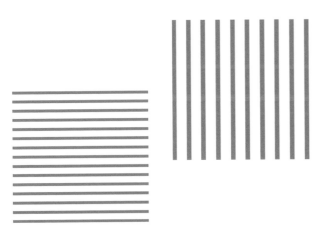

Which set of red lines is wider: A or B?

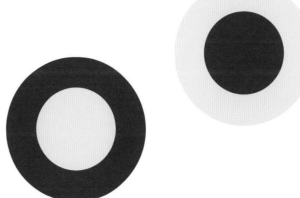

Which middle circle is larger: A or B?

43

Color It!

Seeing Red

Here's one more picture to color all with one color! It looks like a surprise team-up— EraserFace is helping Transmo, and they are on their way back downtown with a batch of mixed-up Animonsters! Red alert! Match markers, colored pencil or crayons to the color swatches below to see more clearly what it is DoodleBug needs to stop!

MATERIALS

colored pencils, markers or crayons in various shades of red

SALMON For the Ostraffe body, Buzzoink stripes, dust cloud, Gorooster face, Transmo glove, eyes, nose tip, license plate, hood flames, and Eraser Face's arm

CARNATION For the light-house beam, Buzzoink's face, Snat's eyes, EraserFace's face and hand, Transmo's brain, the tire rims and bumper teeth

MAGENTA For the sky, Snat, windshield, Eraser-Face's eyes and the car bumpers

RUST For the lava, the tree, Ostraffe's ears, legs, and spots, the background hills, the road, Transmo's face, and Gorooster's body and beak

CARMINE For the rest of the ground and Hot Rod

ROSEWOOD For the smoke, waves, light-house, Transmo's robes, and the tires

SCARLET For the volcano blast, Ostraffe's eyes, Grizzster, the light-house roof, the stop sign, Gorooster's crown and under his eyes and chin, Snat's tongue, the stripe, the fire, and Hot Rod's nose and pupils

Visit impact-books.com/freakyfunactivities to download a free bonus demonstration.

Make It!
SnapDragon

The only way to halt Transmo's Animonster attack is by building an even scarier monster to turn them away! DoodleBug knows most animals are frightened by loud noises and has come up with a plan. Can you help him make a noisy Snapdragon to scare off the strange beasts?

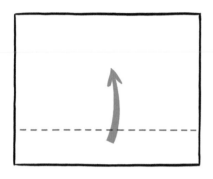 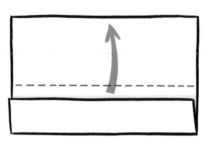 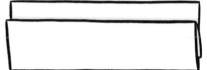

1 Fold the bottom of a piece of regular white paper up around 2" (5cm) as shown. Then fold it up again so it looks like this.

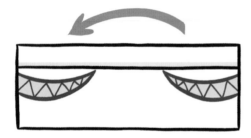 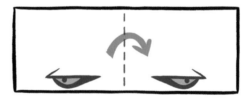 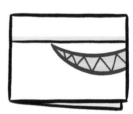

2 Use colored pens, pencils or markers to draw two sets of sharp Snapdragon teeth. Flip the whole thing over. On the other side, draw two spooky Snapdragon eyes near the bottom edge of the paper. Fold the paper in half so it looks like this.

Visit impact-books.com/freakyfunactivities to download a free bonus activity.

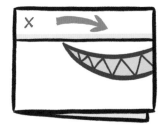 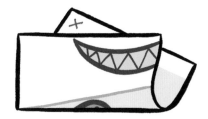

3 This is the hardest part to do. Hold the paper lightly with one hand on the bottom left part beside the drawing of the teeth. Pinch the upper part where the X is with your other hand and pull it across so it looks like this.

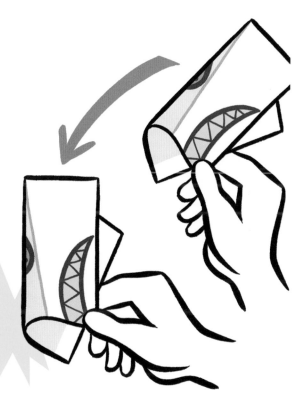

4 When you turn it over, it should look like this. Pinch it tightly at the front under the teeth where the red arrow is pointing.

5 Now SNAP it down quickly as shown. The loud popping sound should be enough to scare off anyone!

Solve It!

Stretchy Maze

Scribble is going to need your help sorting out this stretchy mess. Someone is making a double-terrible mistake in this boxing match, and you need to find out who it is! Using red, yellow and pink markers, colored pencils or crayons, color in the arms of DoodleBug, Transmo and EraserFace to see exactly who is boxing who! (Solution on page 62.)

MATERIALS

red, yellow and pink colored pencils, markers or crayons

I'm going to get you with a stretchy rubber whammer!

Ooh! That looks like fun! I'll transform into something stretchy, too!

Three can play at this game! I'm going to draw out my arms!

This can only end in tears! I can't look!

Make It!

Cosmic Prison

Now that EraserFace has practically defeated himself, it's just down to dealing with Transmo. DoodleBug thinks that Transmo needs a dose of his own medicine— that optical illusions from his own dimension might be able to defeat him! Can you help DoodleBug make a thumatrope illusion to imprison Transmo?

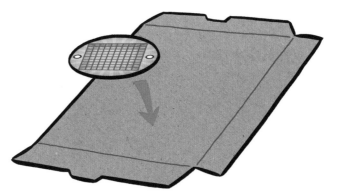

MATERIALS

string

scissors

cardboard

glue or double-sided tape

1 Carefully cut out the two circle images at the bottom of this page. One has a picture of Transmo, and the other, a picture of a cosmic prison.

2 Use glue or double-sided tape to stick the prison circle to a piece of thin cardboard. (Food package cardboard works best.)

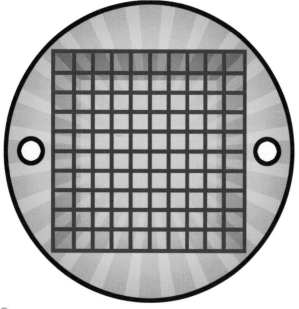

3 When the glue is dry, carefully cut out the prison circle.

4 If you have a hole-punch, carefully punch through the cardboard where the holes are clearly marked. If you don't have a hole-punch, you might need to ask an adult to cut out the holes with a boxcutter or craft knife.

5 Glue or tape the Transmo circle to the other side of the cardboard. Be sure to line up the holes from both sides.

6 Cut two pieces of string about 6"–8" (15cm–20cm) each, and tie one tightly through each hole of the thumatrope.

7 Pull the two strings fairly tight and twist them back and forth between your fingers and thumbs. If you can do this quickly enough while looking at the disc, you will see Transmo appear to be inside the prison! This is due to a trick of the eye called persistence of vision, and it's the perfect trick to trap Transmo!

Draw It!
EraserFace

Now DoodleBug and Scribble have not one, but two trouble-makers to deal with! And EraserFace is tough to defeat because he can un-erase himself back from nothing. Look here he comes!

1 Begin by drawing an oblong shape, slightly taller on the left side.

2 Draw three straight lines to create his side. Add more straight lines to make eyebrows, cheeks and the bottom of his nose. Add one line straight down to separate his legs.

3 Draw two short lines to finish his nose and two more to complete the legs. Add one straight line right across his waist. Make the bottom of both arms V shapes. Add a curved frown.

Visit impact-books.com/freakyfunactivities to download a free bonus activity.

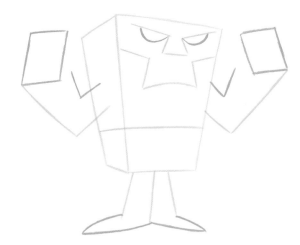

4 Draw his eyes with two wide U shapes. Make his fists with two tilted rectangles. Use smaller V shapes to mark the top of his arms, and curvy V shapes to make his feet.

5 Add little dotted pupils to his eyes. Use small lines to create fingers and thumbs, and add more short lines under his eyes and nose. Add one more short line to make a grumpy eyebrow even grumpier, and another to make the chin. Use curved lines to define his sleeves. Add a letter E on his tummy.

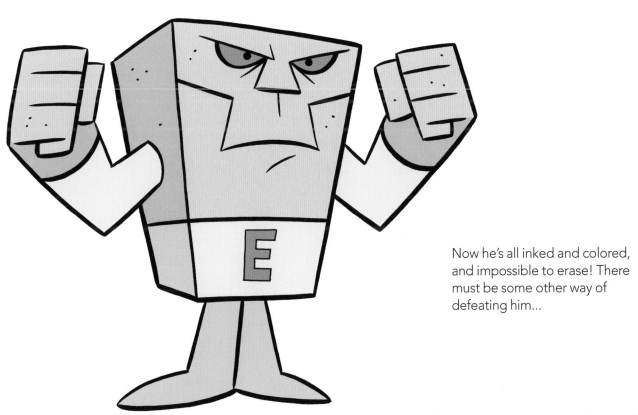

Now he's all inked and colored, and impossible to erase! There must be some other way of defeating him...

Color It!
Colorful Homecoming

Make It!

Flip Faces

Oops! Looks like there's some leftover Transmo power still in town. Cut out these pages along the blue dotted lines to make faces you can mix and mash up by flipping the sections back and forth.

Answer Key

SOLUTION TO PAGE 17: Turn the gnome face upside down to make him smile!

SOLUTION TO PAGE 23: It's Transmo, the inter-dimensional transformer!

SOLUTION TO PAGE 19:

SOLUTION TO PAGES 26–27:

1. Malcolm McGhool isn't see-through.
2. The spider only has seven legs.
3. The lady in the portrait is smiling.
4. The portrait of Capt. A. Ghast is frowning.
5. The portrait of Capt. A. Ghast is missing loops in the frilled collar.
6. There is an extra piece of broken mirror.
7. The circle on the wooden baseboard is missing.
8. The mouse hole is missing.
9. The eye on the fireplace mantle is shut.
10. The wrong fireplace tile is missing.
11. The hole in the sofa is in the wrong place.
12. Capt. A. Ghast's pantaloons are the wrong color.
13. Gross rat is in a different place.

SOLUTION TO PAGE 33: Turn the Sea Sorceress upside down to reveal her true form!

SOLUTION TO PAGE 39: Scribble is in a tree!

SOLUTION TO PAGES 42–43:

1. The two squares are exactly the same size!
2. The three green lines between the arrow points are exactly the same size!
3. The two sets of red lines are exactly the same width and height!
4. The two circles are exactly the same size!

SOLUTION TO PAGE 49: EraserFace is hitting himself twice, and he's so embarrassed he runs home with a headache!

ABOUT THE AUTHOR

Jay Stephens is an award-winning cartoonist, best recognized around the world for his animated television series' *Tutenstein* and *The Secret Saturdays*. Jay is also well known back home in Canada for creating the popular Chick and Dee characters for *chickaDEE Magazine*, as well as co-creating the *Eat It Up! Cookbook for Kids* and *You Crack Me Up! Big Book of Fun* featuring those characters.

Jay currently resides in Guelph, Ontario, where he draws comics, teaches cartoon classes and manages the local art store. To learn more about Jay, please visit jaystephens.com

DEDICATION

This book is dedicated to Hannah, whose ingenious creativity and adventurous spirit is an inspiration to all.

Other fine IMPACT books are available from your favorite bookstore, art supply store or online supplier. Visit our website at fwmedia.com.

18 17 16 15 14   5 4 3 2 1

DISTRIBUTED IN CANADA BY FRASER DIRECT
100 Armstrong Avenue
Georgetown, ON, Canada L7G 5S4
Tel: (905) 877-4411

DISTRIBUTED IN THE U.K. AND EUROPE
BY F&W MEDIA INTERNATIONAL LTD
Brunel House, Forde Close, Newton Abbot
TQ12 4PU, UK
Tel: (+44) 1626 323200, Fax: (+44) 1626 323319
Email: enquiries@fwmedia.com

DISTRIBUTED IN AUSTRALIA BY CAPRICORN LINK
P.O. Box 704, S. Windsor NSW, 2756 Australia
Tel: (02) 4560-1600, Fax: (02) 4577-5288
Email: books@capricornlink.com.au

ISBN: 9781440322143

Edited by Christina Richards
Interior designed by Angela Wilcox
Cover designed by Brianna Scharstein
Production coordinated by Mark Griffin

Metric Conversion Chart

To convert	to	multiply by
Inches	Centimeters	2.54
Centimeters	Inches	0.4
Feet	Centimeters	30.5
Centimeters	Feet	0.03
Yards	Meters	0.9
Meters	Yards	1.1

Visit impact-books.com/freakyfunactivities to download a free bonus demonstration.